The Dirty Secrets The

Mortgage Industry Doesn't

Want You To Know

Marc Savage

National Mortgage Expert

ISBN 978-0-6151-8516-3

Table of Contents

1. Shopping for a Mortgage

Many people would not think of shopping for a mortgage. You spend time saving for the down payment and you diligently shop for the house. The mortgage is that inevitable thing that happens at the end. For those that do shop for a mortgage, they may call a few mortgage companies and ask for a rate. Now, this is a huge mistake and a total waste of your time.

Could you imagine calling up your doctor with a cough? You tell your doctor, "I have this cough. I've got some green phlegm that's been coming out, and I've had this cough for about two days. It's pretty bad. I've been up all night coughing. I need to do something about it," so you ask your doctor, "Can you please give me a prescription for some codeine?"

What do you think your doctor's going to say to you? I need you to come in so I can examine you to figure out what's wrong. You respond to your doctor, "Look, doc, I've had coughs before. I know exactly what's wrong with me. Besides, I've already told you everything you need to know. Just give me the codeine." Your doctor will probably hang up on you because a prescription without diagnosis is malpractice.

So, when you call a mortgage planner and say, "I have a 650 score. I can go full income. I need a $300,000 loan, 30 year fixed rate. What's the rate?" it's basically the same thing. Prescription without diagnosis is malpractice. That's exactly what you're asking a mortgage planner to do. Most people respond the same way, "I just need a rate. I'm shopping around."

I had shoulder surgery a few years ago, and it was costing me a great deal of grief so I had to have my shoulder repaired. So, I called my doctor and asked him who he recommends. He told me Dr. David Dynes. He's the best. So, I did some research on Dr. Dynes and found out he definitely is one of the top doctors in his field. Now, do you think I called up Dr. Dynes and said, "How much is the surgery? What do you charge? I'm shopping around?" Of course not, that's silly.

Although, this is not life and death, it is the single largest transaction you will likely make in your life. I am not advising you to forego research. You should research the market and the planner that you are going to use. I'm just saying that shopping for the rate alone gets you the clinic down the street versus Dr. David Dynes, the top in his field. Believe it or not, there's not going to be a whole lot difference in overall cost between Dr. Dynes and another doctor.

Every mortgage quote is a custom quote. Every situation is different. How long are you keeping the loan? How long are you staying in your home? What are your long term goals? What about income? Do you qualify? You might think you do, but I have had clients surprised. One of my clients was a doctor making over $300,000 a year. Surely, a doctor making this kind of income would qualify full income, right? No, he didn't qualify full income. Why? His monthly payments on all his other debt was just way to high.

Now, he thought he'd qualify full income, but he's a doctor not a mortgage planner. In the same way that I would not necessarily call him and say, "Listen, I know that I don't have a problem with my shoulder," you cannot call a mortgage planner with a self diagnosis.

So, what's the right way to shop for a loan? What are the first steps? Well, first of all, you want to sit down with a professional mortgage planner. With the mortgage planner's specialized help you can discuss your needs, goals and plans. Rather than calling and asking for a rate, you want to design a strategy.

When meeting with the mortgage planner, be prepared with all of your paperwork. You will need two recent pay stubs, two years of W-2s, two years tax returns, and if you're self-employed, it would just be the tax returns. Many times when I meet with clients, I want to do a tax analysis, and that's all part of the overall planning and mortgage cost. The planner will also want to see your bank statements or assets. Prior to your appointment the planner will send you a list of everything he or she might need.

You will next want to get a few options, and you will want to get good faith estimates in writing on all those options. A verbal quote of numbers is meaningless, so make sure to get good faith estimates.

For example, maybe your options include a two year adjustable fixed for two years, a five year adjustable which is fixed for five years or a straight thirty year fixed rate loan. You will want to have good faith estimates on all of these options.

You will also want to consider points. Do you want to pay points? Do you not want to pay points? Points are fees the borrower pays the lender at the time the loan is closed, and it as expressed as a percent of the loan. So if you were taking out a $100,000 loan, 3 points would equal a payment of $3,000. Points are part of the cost of credit to the borrower, and part of the investment return to the lender but they are not mandatory.

Many factors go into considering whether or not you choose to pay points. If you are going to have the loan for a long period of time, then paying points is smart. The points reduce your rate and you will enjoy a lower rate for a longer period of time. Adding to an overall lower total cost for your home loan.

Again, you want to get options and you want it all explained to you. Then, if you want to shop around, you need to do the exact same thing again. Now, that sounds like a lot of work – and it is a lot of work! However, isn't it worth it for the single largest transaction of your life? How much time do you spend planning a vacation? **Most people spend more time planning a vacation than planning their mortgage**

So, why don't more people shop for a loan? Well, it's too much trouble, too much work, and really, who has the time. Look, we all spend all day at work. We get home, and we want to relax. That gives us our weekends. Well, on the weekends, we need to go with the kids to hockey practice or soccer practice, or we just want some down time, totally understandable. Maybe you want to spend some time with your wife.

My wife, Wendy, is constantly telling me that I don't spend enough time with her, and in fairness, she's probably right, but she certainly doesn't want to spend that time planning a mortgage. In her case, she doesn't have to because she's stuck with a mortgage planner as a husband. (That could be a whole other book "Diary of a neglected wife")

So, most people try to find the easiest way to shop around and that is make a bunch of phone calls looking for the lowest rate. Or perhaps, you use the internet and shop for rate quotes online. However, shopping on price alone (lowest rate) is a guaranteed formula for getting burned. I have heard from hundreds of people who were promised one thing and got another. So in light of this who do we ask for advice? We turn to our parents, friends, co-workers, and other family members- the people we trust. We do not ask for a referral because they got burned too. Instead we ask them what kind of mortgage to obtain. What's a good rate? Should I pay points?

The scary part of all of this is how the heck would they know? How many mortgages have they done - one, two, or maybe three? I've personally helped more than 1,357 people get home loans. What that means to you is I have the experience to help you find the best loan for your needs. Your friends, your family, your co-workers, they don't have that experience. So, you're asking the people that you're most comfortable in asking, but they can't possibly have all the knowledge to guide you in this process.

Again, you want to ask the professionals, not somebody who has a mortgage or two. When you have a plumbing problem, you call a plumber not a roofer. The roofer may be perfectly skilled at his job. He may be trustworthy and reasonably priced but unless he is also a plumber he's not the best choice to repair your pipes. Your mortgage is important and getting specialized help will get you the best information and help you avoid pitfalls. Not only is your mortgage the single largest transaction you will ever make but it's also potentially the longest! Shouldn't you spend some time designing it and planning it, not just making a couple of phone calls to shop for a rate? Besides, if it's not in writing, it's absolutely worthless.

How could it be too much trouble to do it right? If you do it wrong, it's more trouble, it's more expensive, especially if you get burned and you find out the real story at closing.   If you didn't know you were getting a two year adjustable mortgage that is not designed properly, that's almost guaranteed to go up, you're going to have to refinance in two years. Did you save money by getting the lowest rate? Did you save money by going with the wrong person? Of course not, it cost you more money.

You need to find the right planner. I advise that you only work with a member of NARLO, the National Association of Responsible Loan Officers. You can learn about NARLO by going to my website, www.yourhomeyourmoney.org, and clicking on the NARLO logo at the bottom of the screen. I am not only a founding member of NARLO I am also an acting board member.

You also want to avoid working with anyone who doesn't need at least thirty minutes of your time to sit with you and go over a plan, whether it's in person, which is always preferable, or over the phone. If a mortgage planner is unwilling to spend time with you they're not looking to help you out. They're just looking to make a fast buck at your expense. Think about it. The faster I get you off the phone and sell you a loan, the faster I move on to the next person. So, who am I helping? I'm helping me, not you. That's **not** the way to do it.

A good mortgage planner will help you plan the financing of your biggest asset, your home. In fact a good mortgage planner will not want to work with a client who doesn't want to devote the time to the process and provide the information needed to give them proper advice. Their interest is in getting the job done right not fast.

Personally, I won't even work with anyone who won't come to my office for a consultation. Why won't I do it over the phone like all the other loan officers out there? Because I want to spend the time with you focusing on your wants and needs. Not with you being interrupted by normal everyday life at home or work.

Ask the Right Questions

When shopping for a mortgage, whether a new mortgage or refinance, there are a few basic questions that you and the lender should be asking.

1. How long are you planning to stay in the home? This answer will determine if you should pay points for a lower rate, whether or not a prepayment penalty makes sense (a prepayment penalty might give you a lower rate because the lender knows you'll be in the loan for a certain amount of time) and whether you should opt for a fixed or adjustable rate mortgage.

2. How much will the loan cost? Your good faith estimate should provide a breakdown of estimated lending costs for appraisals, credit reports, document preparation, origination and discount fees, title insurance, pest inspection and more. There will also be an "estimated cash at closing" line. Keep in mind that these are estimates but you should compare

estimated fees between lenders. I offer a closing cost guarantee with my Good Faith Estimate

3. How long will it take me to recoup the costs? For a new loan how long will it take you to break even if you pay points to get a lower rate? If you are refinancing your mortgage how long will take you to recoup the closing costs from your monthly savings. If it will take you 6 years to break even but you only plan to remain in the home for four years, then the "savings" may not be worth it.

4. How good is my credit? Your credit determines the rate for which you will qualify. The better your credit, the lower the rate. So, if you have a blemished credit record you may not qualify for the quoted rate. Check your credit report before you shop for a mortgage, and correct any inaccuracies. If your credit is really damaged, take time to rebuild it before buying a home.

5. How long should I lock in a rate? You may need to lock in a rate for 45 days as opposed to 30 days. If interest rates are on the rise and you're dealing with a busy loan office you may want to lock in the rate for a longer period of time.

6. Can I afford the payments? When all is said and done, you will need to make the mortgage payments every month for years to come. Your budget should not be stretched to the limit to make the payments. You will also need to budget in savings. Repairs on your home are inevitable and a savings

cushion will prevent you from going into debt if the roof leaks or you need a new hot water heater.

Overview of Loan Types

While there are a number of different types of loan programs the basic loan types are listed below.

Fixed-Rate Mortgage -A mortgage loan program where the interest rate does not change for the life of the loan, so for example in a 30 year fixed loan, your interest rate remains the same for the entire 30 year period.

Adjustable Rate Mortgage (ARM) -A mortgage loan program in which the interest rate is adjusted periodically based on an index. This is also called a variable rate mortgage and is covered in depth in a later chapter.

Balloon Mortgage – This type of mortgage is a fixed-rate mortgage loan for a set number of years (usually five or seven) and then must be paid off in full in a single "balloon" payment. So you can have a 30 year loan term but after the fixed period, you can refinance or make the balloon payment. Balloon mortgage loan programs are popular with those expecting to sell or refinance their property within a definite period of time.

Two-Step Mortgage -A mortgage loan program where the interest rate is fixed for the first seven years and then is adjusted one time for the balance of the loan period.

Conforming Loan -A mortgage loan program for up to and including $417,000 in the continental United States (Alaska and Hawaii limits are higher).

Jumbo Loan -A mortgage loan program for $417,001 or more in the continental United States (Alaska and Hawaii limits are higher). These limits are set by the Federal National Mortgage Association and the Federal Home Loan Mortgage Corporation. Because jumbo loans cannot be funded by these two agencies, they usually carry a higher interest rate.

Predatory Lending

Many people think that the cheapest mortgage is the best mortgage, but the reality is that the *right* mortgage is the best mortgage. Getting the cheapest thirty year fixed rate loan is going to cost you a lot more money if a thirty year fixed rate loan is not the right loan for you. Shopping for the cheapest mortgage has exposed many potential home owners to predatory lending practices.

What exactly is predatory lending? Predatory lending is a practice where lenders try to fool you or even bully you into taking out a loan that's really unaffordable or not in your best interest. These lenders are simply seeking to make a profit and unfortunately it's at your expense.

Predatory lending has been receiving national attention due to the current economic conditions in the real estate industry. It is estimated that as of this writing approximately $9.1 billion per year has been lost to predatory lending. These lending practices typically take advantage of the elderly, minorities, and people with credit issues.

Another ugly side of predatory lending is outright fraud, where documents are signed for borrowers without their knowledge. Borrowers have discovered that something was signed for them, and they had no clue. They never knew about it.

Online lending has been a significant source of predatory practices. Buyers go online to find the cheapest rate. After finding the desired low rate at a lending website they are promised a certain rate and loan type, only to find out the truth when they get to closing.

You start out with one rate and one type of loan, for example, maybe you were offered a six percent interest rate. You get to closing and you find that it's six and a half percent, seven percent, or maybe higher. You're looking at a thirty year fixed, but you end up with an adjustable.

Some predatory lenders may advertise that they have no fee loans. However they engage in an underhanded game of semantics by calling the fees charges or burying them in other aspects of the loans. You may also be told that there will be no closing costs but when it's time to close you end up paying costs. To avoid these practices, it's important to always obtain a good faith estimate in writing, and ask questions about everything.

Good faith estimates should break down everything you will be expected to pay. You want to be careful and go item by item over any good faith estimate with any loan officer, mortgage company, or planner. Ask if they offer a guarantee

Unfortunately, many people spend more time planning a vacation than researching a mortgage. Your mortgage is usually the single largest transaction of your life, and should be given more attention than thirty seconds on a phone call just to get a price. Finding out the rate over the phone or the internet does not begin to cover the amount of information you need to find the best mortgage for you.

Now, another game played with predatory lending is pre-payment penalties. A prepayment penalty is an additional fee if you pay the loan off early. An early pay off would include refinancing as you are paying off your existing loan and taking out a new one.

Predatory lenders will typically not disclose pre-payment penalties and borrowers find out when they are looking to pay the loan off soon. In recent years this has become a significant problem. Many borrowers tried to refinance out of adjustable rate mortgages at the end of their introductory rate period. These borrowers discovered that there was a prepayment penalty. The penalty combined with the decline in housing prices made a refinance impossible because they could not qualify for a loan large enough to cover their payoff and penalties in a soft market.

Prepayment penalties are not an unscrupulous practice on its own. Now, if you don't know about it, and you find out at your next refinance or your next closing, that's predatory lending.

Pre payment penalties may be more than a year. For example, in New York by state law, you can only have a one year prepayment penalty on a fixed rate mortgage. On an adjustable rate mortgage, it has to be a $250,000 mortgage or greater to have a one year prepayment penalty but federal chartered savings banks don't fall under New York State law. So, they can charge a prepay penalty of anything they want.

So, if your broker, or your lender, happens to be working with a federally chartered bank, you may be subject to a three year or five year prepayment penalty, and you don't even know about it.

The next big predatory lending trick is hiding the balloon payment. What is a balloon payment? A balloon payment mortgage is one in which the mortgage does not fully amortize over the term of the note leaving a balance due at maturity. For example, you may have a thirty year loan for $100,000. You make payments on the loan for three to seven years, and at the end of that time period you might owe a balance of $95-$98,000. Well, that's due and payable. It's actually like a payment coupon that shows a $95,000 balance.

Some balloon payment mortgages have reset options, which mean that at the end of the period the mortgage resets to a fully amortized schedule using current market rates. However this option is not automatic and is not typical in the cases of predatory loans. So, what are you going to do when you get a balloon payment bill? You have two options - refinance or come up with the cash, or you risk losing your home to foreclosure. The bottom line is that's a trick that you didn't know about, and you didn't find out about it until it was way too late. Again, that's predatory lending.

Here's an example (Mary asked that her full name not be used)

Mary had done two previous loans with me and came to me for a third loan. She was always happy with my service. When she called me for her third loan, I offered her at the time a thirty year fixed rate loan, with a rate of 6 1/2 % and I was charging two points. She got a call from another loan officer whom she did not know and he offered her 6.2% thirty year fixed, zero points, and lower closing costs.

I knew there was no way that my client could possibly have gotten a loan with that kind of pricing. So, I asked her: "Why don't you send me the good faith estimate, and let's take a look at it and see what's happening." She said she was waiting for the good faith estimate to be sent to her. I said, "Okay, well, let's put the appraisal on hold," because we were moving forward we had ordered an appraisal. "Let's put the appraisal on hold, and we'll see what happens when that new good faith comes in from the other lender, with the other person." I didn't hear back from her until…

About a year later, I got a phone call. She called me to refinance. I said, "Well, why are you refinancing now? What happened?" She said "Well, that 6.2% rate that they promised I received but it turned out to be a two year adjustable rate, and by the way, the no point loan? I paid three points."

Mary had worked with a lender not a broker, which is certainly not shocking. The lender told here there were no broker fees (true), no origination fees (also true) and no points (partially true). However lenders can charge discount points. So, they charged her three discount points.

Mary's story, while sad is not only true…It is unfortunately not an uncommon one. Mary never got a good faith estimate, although having one is not a guarantee. In rare cases you can have a good faith estimate and still be subjected to lies. However it's not common that a lender or broker is going to put a good faith estimate in writing, and lie, but it happens. All the more reason for you to deal with trusted professionals.

To avoid predatory lending, ask the right questions and use the right people. Use a trusted professional who will not simply quote you a rate but will ask you for information so they can get you the right loan.

Predatory lenders do not represent the whole profession but it's important that consumers perform their due diligence when shopping for a mortgage. These lenders take advantage of those who feel they have no other choice. If something sounds too good to be true more than likely you're right!

An ethical lender is not only going to disclose information but ask you for information. No one can quote you a rate without knowing more about you and your specific needs. Once you sign the loan documents it's too late, so take the extra time on the front end to make sure you really are getting the best mortgage for you.

Preparing for a Mortgage

Before you shop for a mortgage you must prepare to have one. This is a crucial step that many miss. Creating a budget to manage your money is very important, but it's something that most people never do. The reasons range from not knowing how to do a monthly budget, to believing there is no need. Every household *should* have a budget, but it becomes critical when you are considering a mortgage or a refinance.

A budget is simply a tool to better manage your money. Having a budget does not mean that you can never go out for dinner or buy a new pair of shoes. A budget allows you to plan your expenses so that you can afford the life you want. There are many books, online tools and resources for budget planning so I will not go into great detail here. The first step in planning a budget is to determine how you are currently spending your money.

You can start to plan your budget my making two lists for expenses. The first list should include your monthly expenses such as mortgage or rent, utility bills, and insurance payments. The second list should include discretionary or non-recurring expenses such as clothing, car maintenance, etc. The next step is to list your income. Now you will review where you are today? Do you have monthly shortfalls? Are you spending more than you desire or worse, more than you actually make?

In reviewing your budget, you should also include a review of your insurance. At least once per year meet with all of your financial professionals including your insurance agent to review your needs and make any adjustments if necessary. For example, you may be able to raise your deductible to save money or combine policies. Your insurance agent can sit down with you and make sure that your policies meet your current needs.

As you review your budget it's important to understand debt. Not all debt is bad. Mortgage debt is considered good debt, while credit card debt is definitely bad debt. You are gaining a return on your mortgage and the interest that you pay is likely smaller than that you incur with credit cards. With credit card debt you increase the amount that you spend on items due to the interest and finance charges.

In your budget planning your first step is to seek ways to eliminate any credit card debt. How can you do that? Look at your expenses and find ways that you can cut expenses and apply the savings to your credit card debt. There are many easy ways to cut down on expenses such as changing or combing phone and/or cell phone plans, downgrading your cable or satellite TV plan, and practicing energy efficiency in your home.

I've found that clients can save over $100 per month on cable or satellite tv alone. You have the top premier package because the salesperson shows you what a huge savings it is versus paying for each individual package, but you never really use the other parts of the package. Review your service package and see what you don't use and where you can cut back.

You can save money on your energy bill with a few small changes. Unplug appliances when they're not in use. Most people do not realize that even though an appliance is not on, if it's plugged in it's still using energy. So unplug those cell phone adapters, blow dryers, toasters and even lamps when they are not in use. Many of the environmental tips are not only eco-friendly but budget friendly as well.

You can save money on your heating bill by installing a digital thermostat. If you live in a cold weather state, during the winter you can't leave your heat completely off when you're not in home, but you can lower the thermostat. An adjustable thermostat enables you to set the heat to a lower temperature when you're not at home. When you're at home you can also set the thermostat a little lower and wear a sweater, sweatshirt or warm clothing. Just a few degrees lower makes a huge difference in your bill.

Now for the dreaded credit cards. How many credit cards do you have? Write down each card, and the total amount owed and the interest rate. Reducing your credit card debt might be a little more complicated, unfortunately because there are just so many options available to you. It depends really how many you have and how much money you owe and how much money you have at the end of the month to possibly pay extra towards your credit cards.

Now, if you have enough money, you can look to just make extra payments to get these debts paid off, and this, many times, can be the absolute cheapest way to go. In this scenario, attack the highest interest rate card first. You will continue making payments on all cards but you'll apply extra to the card with the highest interest rate. When this is paid off you take the money you were paying on that card and apply it to the next highest interest rate card.

One of the problems, however with credit card debt is that you've been overspending for so long, you can barely make minimum payments as it is. So, it really might be difficult or even impossible to pay anything extra to pay them off sooner.

You can call the credit card companies and try to negotiate lower rates. In some cases, the credit card companies will have a willingness to lower your interest rate, but with the new bankruptcy laws, many of them just won't do it.

Now, there's consumer credit counseling which in some cases can help you negotiate lower rates and payments, but you really need to be extremely careful with this path because not all of these companies are reputable, and they don't make your payments on time, and that can hurt you as much as anything else.

See, with many of these counseling companies, they negotiate for you and get improved terms, which is not a bad thing obviously.

Then, you pay them one monthly payment, and they disperse it out to the credit card companies. The problem here is while you might pay the credit counseling company on time, they may not pay your creditors on time, and that shows up on your credit report as a late payment. So, again be very careful. I've experienced a number of these situations with past clients who were in credit counseling. They have direct withdrawal right out of their bank statements, so they can see that they're making those payments right to the credit counseling agency and the bills are paid late. Not because they paid late, but because the agency paid late or the consumer credit counseling agency paid late.

Finally, there is of course, consolidating your debt, credit card and or car loans. There are two ways to do this. One is with a personal loan. Now, I don't do personal loans, but I have actually helped clients use personal loans in the past. One particular client I helped used a personal loan of $30,000 to consolidate his and his wife's credit card debt. This personal loan lowered his overall rates and monthly payments. They were able to save $500 a month, and they used that savings to accelerate the payoff of the debt, and they were debt free in two years, which then helped them to qualify to buy a home.

Now, the other way of course is with a mortgage refinance. This more often than not is the least expensive and most affordable route for a homeowner. When you're in over your head, and you have so much credit card debt, it's probably impossible to find the extra money to accelerate the payoff.

Also, even with consumer credit counseling or a lower rate, the monthly payments might still be out of reach. By consolidating this personal debt into what most likely will be tax deductible mortgage debt, you will get a lower overall rate in payment. By creating this type of payment relief, we can find ways to utilize that extra monthly money to your benefit, by accelerating your mortgage payoff, creating a savings account or a host of other benefits.

The budgeting process is not that difficult. While there are certain expenses that you cannot get rid of, such as your utility bills but you can find ways to lower expenses and better manage your money.

Debt and Credit

It seems that more and more Americans are falling behind on their debt. This is not just mortgages and subprime borrowers. People are falling behind on credit cards, car loans and overdraft lines of credit. And things do not look like they are going to get better any time soon.

So what is the underlying cause of this increasing delinquency on all different types of debt? You may have already guessed it's the slowing housing market. You see when the housing market was on fire, Americans were using their homes like giant ATM machines.

People would go out, buy themselves anything and everything they could get their hands on and just charge it to the ole' credit card. When they ran out of room on their credit cards they would call around and shop for a mortgage. You know…a bunch of phone calls to get the lowest rate. The just refinance all that debt into a nice new low rate mortgage.

The booming housing market was basically carrying the economy. While wages were failing to keep up with inflation, people needed a way to continue to buy, buy, buy. Every year homeowners found a huge deposit of new equity in their favorite ATM. So off they went to take out some more spending money.

It was the best of times. Interest rates were low, the housing market just kept going up and up and up. Like the "New Economy" many people thought the housing boom was never going to end. But, just like the "New Economy" every market has cycles and the housing market came to the end of its upward cycle.

Now when someone finds themselves to be tapped out on their credit cards they no longer can look to their home for those big equity deposits. In some cases where housing prices have dropped, many homeowners are seeing an unexpected withdrawal of equity from their favorite ATM.

With no additional equity in their home to help them refinance their debt, many homeowners can't make their monthly debt payments. We saw most of the problem in the subprime mortgage market, but now we are hearing rumblings of delinquencies in the prime mortgage market.

Delinquencies on consumer credit, such as credit cards and car loans are going to spike up in the coming months. When a homeowner has less money coming in than going out, they start to rob from Peter to pay Paul. In most cases homeowners pay their mortgage first and everything else second.

Debt Consolidation

A lot of people think that debt consolidation is saving money, but really lowering your payments isn't saving money. Saving money is saving money.

With debt consolidation you are really just moving your debt around. So, you take your credit card debts, you car loans, your personal loan, your overdraft lines of credit, all your different debts, mostly non-deductible non-tax deductible debts, and you combine them with your mortgage.

Of course, there are advantages. You will likely get a lower interest rate. Most credit cards are 12, 16, 18, 20% versus a mortgage at six or seven percent. You also have the opportunity to lower your monthly payments and of course you have now combined all of your debt into a tax deductible vehicle.

Now, when we talk about various types of debt, there's two basic types of debt – good debt, and bad debt. I know you're thinking, "Good debt, there's no such thing as good debt." Well, when you look at overall debt, there is a big difference between the two types of debt.

For example, credit cards usually have a higher interest rate than most other types of debt. In addition, credit cards aren't tax deductible. Car loans are generally not tax deductible either. Now, a lot of people say, "Well, my car loan is cheaper than a mortgage."

You may be able to get a car loan at five percent, where your mortgage rate might be six percent. However what people fail to take into consideration is the tax deduction. On a 6% mortgage you may get back 2% on your tax return resulting in an overall rate of 4%.

When you do a debt consolidation loan you may assume that you're saving money and are in a much better financial position. For example, you may have consolidated $3,000 of monthly mortgage, credit card debt, car loan payments and more to a new lower payment of $2,000. So, it's a thousand dollars savings, and that's great. But lowering your monthly payments is only step 1 of the process.

Here's the reality. If you consolidated all this debt, and you lower your payments by $1,000 a month and you continue with the same spending habits, you're going to end up right back where you were before.

Now, some people don't want to consolidate debt on their mortgage or put it on the house, because they don't want to use up the equity in their house. While this is true, let's consider the alternative. Let's assume that your home is worth $500,000 house. Your mortgage is $200,000 mortgage, and you have $50,000 in credit card debt. Your net worth is $500,000 minus $200,000 minus $50,000 or $250,000. Unless you plan on selling your house and filing bankruptcy and hiding the money in your backyard which, you no longer own, by the way, how are you getting rid of that debt? You can't get rid of the debt because you can't file bankruptcy to get rid of it. So, what are you doing?

Some people say, "Well, when I sell the house, I'll pay the debt off." Okay, so, let's see. What we're going to do is we're going to go out and we're going to continue paying high interest rates. We're not going to get a tax benefit so that when we sell the house, we can pay off the debt. Not to mention, what happens if the market experiences a downturn and your house drops in value? Debt is debt. It doesn't matter where the debt is, and some debt is better than other debt. If you have to have the debt, have it in the right places.

Debt consolidation is not a bad strategy and combined with a change in spending habits it can truly lead to financial freedom. Let's get debt free. Use the savings to accelerate your mortgage payoff or increase your wealth.

Home equity is the number one source of wealth in this country. That's not necessarily a good statement. It's just a true statement. A good statement would be, "Savings is the number one source of wealth in this country," but this is simply not the case.

In our example, we lowered monthly payments from $3000 to $2000 which frees up $1000 per month. We can now take that $1000 and invest it in a retirement plan or other investment vehicle. In this way you are using your monthly savings to build wealth.

You could also take the savings and fund your children's education. Most parents have some sort of plan, but what's the plan? Maybe they put $10 away in the piggy bank. Most parents, most families don't have a real plan for their children's education, unfortunately. Creating an education fund can prevent your children from starting their adult lives off saddled with student loan debt. Of course you could just send that extra $1,000 per month to your mortgage company and pay off your home faster than you ever dreamed possible

Finally, the last part of debt consolidation is an annual review. You will want to check in with your financial planner and review your situation. Where are you now and how does it compare to where you were previously? Where are you going and are you on the right road to get there. What kind of changes have you had in your life? Have you had any kids? Have you had any grandkids? Are your kids in college? Are we on the right course?

Life changes in a split second. A year later, the world is changed. It's important to check in to make sure that you're doing everything to remain on the right path.

Credit Scores and Mortgage

Let's talk a little bit about credit scores specifically. Credit scores range from 350 to 850. Everybody knows about credit scores or what's called a FICO score. FICO is only one of the types of credit scoring systems but it is the most widely known.

Your credit score however is not the only factor in getting a loan. A lot of people just call around shopping for the best rate, and then they say, "We have a score of blah, blah," and what's the rate?

The bottom line is a score of X doesn't tell enough of a story. There are a lot of other factors. Sometimes a high score may not qualify for a conforming loan or for some of the better loan programs, and sometimes that high score can be misleading. You may have late payments or other issues that aren't really shown in the score.

Conversely, low scores sometimes do qualify, and as with high scores the number does not tell the whole story. Sometimes, you may have a low score, and you don't have any late payments or you don't have any late mortgage payments – and a late mortgage payment, when you're going to get a mortgage is more important than late credit card payments.

While scores are not the only factor they are a very important component so I want to ensure you understand them. There are score ranges. Now, these are very general rules, and each situation is different. So, again, remember, general rules here.

If you have a score from 720 to 850, that's excellent credit. You're probably going to fit into the best rates and best programs, again other factors apply such as income, assets and loan to value but a range of 720 to 850 is an excellent score. In this range you should not have too much trouble getting a loan of any sort.

A range of 680-719 is very good credit, and again, you're going to fit into most of the best rates and programs.

Many good programs are available in the 620-679 score, but you may or may not fit into conforming. You may or may not fit into some of the best products so 620-679 is one of those gray areas.

A range of 560-619 is considered fair credit. It's also known as sub-prime credit. Now, I don't like calling it sub-prime. It sounds like you're almost like sub-human. I like to call it non-conforming. You're not sub anything, and there are many good programs available including 100% financing with a 560 through 619 score. Your rate's going to be slightly higher than conforming, maybe one or two percent higher than a conforming loan, but certainly not much more than that.

A range of 500-559 is considered a very high credit risk. Again, it's called sub-prime and there are still a number of programs available, but the rates are usually over two percent higher than a conforming loan.

If you're below 500, it's very difficult to find mortgage financing. There are very few programs available. While not impossible to find a loan it is a lot tougher in this credit range and you will not qualify for the best programs. There is however hope. I specialize in helping people who had a bankruptcy or other credit challenge get affordable mortgage loans. I actually have a program called the get mortgage ready program. So, if you fall into the category of below 500, 500-559, if you just feel that you're not there, not where you need to be there is help and it's possible for you to obtain a mortgage.

Now, remember these are general rules. They're not etched in stone. As an industry we understand that sometimes bad things happen to good people. A few years ago, I personally had some credit problems, so I totally know where people with credit problems are coming from.

I had some income issues. I got pretty deep into debt, and my scores were under 550. So, I do understand what it's like. I had trouble getting any kind of financing or any kind of loans at that time, and here I am in the mortgage business. You say I should've known better, but it's not a matter of knowing better. I had problems. Things happen. Bad things happen to good people, and I ran into that problem. Because I've been there I understand how it can happen. There's no need to be embarrassed if this is your situation.

The Nature of Scoring

Now that you understand scores, what affects your credit scores? Payment history is 35% of your overall credit score. So, for example, if you have late payments, obviously that's a negative on your credit, and if you have timely payments, that's good on your credit. The age of the late payments is also very important.

So, in other words, the older your late payments are, the less they affect your credit. The more recent your late payments are, the worse it affects your credit. If you're late today, that's worse than if you were late twelve months ago, 24 months ago, or years ago.

The way lenders look at it, it's much more important how you pay today than how you paid yesterday. The fact that you paid perfectly a year ago, is not as important as paying perfectly today.

The type of credit that was late also has an impact. For example if you have a very high payment that's going to affect a line of credit or whatever that credit might be, that's going to impact your scores more than a very low payment. Car payments, mortgage payments, things like that are going to affect your credit much more greatly.

There's a lot of confusion about late payments. Many people think that they were late because they paid after the grace period and they had a late fee. That's not necessarily late as far as credit scoring is concerned.

Here's how late payments are graded. You have late periods of 30 days 60 days, 90 days, 120 days and 120 days and over 120 days. Thirty days later means that you did not pay within 30 days of your due date. So, if you were due on the first of September and you paid October 1st, that's a 30 day late.

You also have to catch up completely or you're going to stay late. So, in other words, if you were late sixty days and make one payment, you're now thirty days late. If you keep making your monthly payments form that point forward, you stay thirty days late.

Believe it or not, it's actually worse from a credit grading standpoint, at least as a mortgage company to have a thirty day late, then get current, and then go thirty days late again. It's actually better to stay thirty days late providing your lender allows it. I'm not proposing that anybody should stay late. It's not a good thing.

But, we have found from a grading standpoint that if you stay thirty days late, it's better than flip flopping between being thirty days late and then current and thirty days late again. In fact some lenders will count six months or more of 30 day late in a row. So, if you were late every month for thirty days, that's what we call a rolling thirty, and it's actually better than a record that reads:

Jan – 30 days late, Feb - current, Mar – 30 days late, April – current, May – 30 days late

because the pattern of late, current, late, current adds up three thirty day late payments. If you did that over twelve months, that would be six thirty day late payment versus twelve months straight of thirty day lates, which would be considered one by some lenders.

So, again, I'm not proposing staying late ever. You always want to pay your bills on time, but current, late, current, late is worse than staying thirty days late.

The next big contributing factor to scores are balances. Balances are 30% of your overall credit. So, balances are based on each individual card, or each individual line and your overall credit.

Let's say for example you have a credit card and you owe 30% of that line. So, you have a $10,000 credit limit, and you owe $3,000. That would be a 30% balance and that's the best, 30% and less. If you're 50% or $5,000, it's still okay, but it's not as good at 30%. If you owe $10,000 on that $10,000 line, that's a negative.

For example, if you have one $10,000 credit line that's maxed out, but you have ten other credit lines and they're all zero, and they're all $10,000 lines of credit that is no big deal. There's certainly a negative to the one line being maxed out, but not that horrible because your overall credit is $100,000.00 and you've used $10,000.00 of what's available to you.

On the other hand if you have one line of credit of $10,000 and that's maxed out, and you have another line of credit for $10,000 and that's zero, your 50% overall max plus you're maxed out on a line. That's actually a bad thing.

New installment credit – car loan, mortgage loan, things like that, where you are technically maxed out as soon as you take out the loan are viewed differently than credit card debt. You're not in a cycle of borrow-pay-borrow again. When the loan is paid off it's paid.

These first two factors are 65% of your overall score, 65% of your overall score. They're the most important factors. The other three factors basically contribute 35% and it's broken up into 15%, 10%, and 10%.

The age of your credit accounts for 15%. So, what's the age of your credit? For example, if you have a lot of lines of credit and they're all closed, so you have no open lines of credit, really the problem is you have no recent history of your ability to repay or to manage debt.

If you have lot of new lines that are all open with zero balances, again, you have no real recent history of ability to manage your debt. If you have a lot of open lines that are open two years or more, then you have plenty of recent history of ability to manage debt. It doesn't mean it's good ability. You might manage your debt horribly, but nonetheless, we have depth of credit and history and that would account for 15% of your overall score.

The type of credit you have accounts for 10%. Mortgage and installment debt are your best type of debt. The next best type of debt if you're going to have credit card debt is major credit cards – Master, Visa, American Express, Diner's Card, cards like that, would be your next best type of credit.

From a credit scoring standpoint the worse kind of credit you can have is store cards. Don't misunderstand. That doesn't necessarily mean that having a JC Penny card or a Macy's card or any of these cards is bad. Don't run out and cancel your cards because it's "bad". It's not bad to have them. It's just bad as an overall type of credit. It's only ten percent of your overall score, and certainly if you have plenty of other credit – installment loans, car loans, mortgages, credit cards, then it's not going to have a major impact. The key is to have a good mix of major credit cards, mortgage and installment debt.

Inquiries are about ten percent of your overall credit grade and is the least understood of all the factors. A lot of loan officers, lenders, brokers, use it to scare borrowers from shopping and what they'll say is don't let anybody else run your credit. It's going to hurt your score. That's partially true, but it's also to a great extent not true. I'm going to get to that.

Remember, inquiries are only ten percent of your overall score. So, if you have a maximum score of 850, then the maximum it can affect your score is 85 points. Inquiries can affect your score from two points per inquiry to 25 points per inquiry. The maximum number of inquiries you can have that will affect your score in any six month period is ten. So, if you have 10 inquiries in six months or 100 inquiries in 6 months it counts the same.

Mortgage and auto loan inquiries are completely different than credit card inquiries. When you want to shop for a mortgage or installment loan like a car loan, the lender or broker will need the credit score to make an offer. Well, how can you shop around for a loan if every inquiry affects your score? You can't.

Well, here's the part that probably 99-100% of loan officers out there don't know. It's what I call the 14 day rule. The 14 day rule says, you can have an unlimited number of inquiries mortgage and installment inquiries in 14 days and it counts as one inquiry – So if run your credit for a mortgage today, you have 14 days to run it an unlimited number of times and it only counts as one inquiry. On day 15 the count down starts all over again and you now have 2 inquiries.

Again, this is really the most absolute misunderstood of all the factors in overall credit scoring. Banks, brokers, loan officers, they all use it to scare you from shopping for a loan. Again, I'm not saying that shopping around is the smartest thing to do, but certainly if you're going to shop around, know the rules and make sure whatever you do, when you shop around, you get in writing. You get a good faith estimate, and it's all in writing. You can't get that without somebody running your credit.

So, when a loan officer, a bank or broker says, 'Don't let anybody run your credit, it's going to hurt your score,' you can answer, "You know what? That's true, but I know the fourteen day rule." I guarantee you whoever you're speaking to says, "What fourteen day rule?"

Again, remember, you can run an unlimited number of inquiries for a mortgage or installment loan, unlimited in fourteen days, and it counts as one. It starts from the first inquiry.

Raising your Scores

What can you do to bring up your score and do it quickly? Well, pay down open high balance credit cards. Redistribute your debt. For example, if you have a $10,000 line of credit, it's maxed out $10,000, and you have some other credit cards that have some free availability, distribute it out. Bring everything down to 30% if you can. Certainly, if you can't bring it down to 30% make it 50%.

Don't close these cards out. If you close out your cards, you limit your availability to borrow, and you actually hurt your credit. A lot of people don't understand that. It's depth of credit and the amount of balances. If you have one credit card and that's it, then there's not a whole depth of credit there.

The first and foremost thing you can do to bring your credit up and bring it up quickly is to bring yourself current. If you're delinquent on anything, do your best to bring yourself current. That'll certainly bring your scores up and it'll do it fast.

Longer term there are certain things that just time is the only thing that's going to help you bring your credit score up. So, if you don't have enough accounts, you have to go out and get some new credit card accounts in order to build depth.

If you have late payments, again, only patience is going to get you home there. You need time for those payments to age. Remember, the more recent a late payment, the worse it is. The older a late payment, the better it is.

People get themselves into trouble, and when they do, they're not sure what to pay, who to pay, and when to pay it. The bottom line is the first and foremost thing you always pay – always, always, always – I can't emphasize that enough is your mortgage. Why? First of all, it's the roof over your head. If you pay your car, or credit cards, do you really want to live in your car and get evicted from your house or get foreclosed on your house and live in the street? Of course, not. Give up your car, your credit cards and have a place to live.

As a matter of fact, a lot of people, will look at their credit cards, and these are all small payments. They feel like they can make them. They make them and then they don't pay their mortgage.

Some lenders will give you a mortgage even if you have under a 500 score. If you remember what I said, under 500 is real tough. But…even if you have under a 500 score, as long as your mortgage history is perfect, the odds of you getting a loan that will benefit you are good. So when your funds are tight, make the mortgage a priority and pay it on time. Let me give you an example…

James had some real credit issues. He had an existing loan of $387,000, a seven percent interest rate, thirty year term, and a

*payment of $2574 that he was not escrowing for taxes and insurance.
So, he had to pay that on his own.*

*He had credit cards and car loans of $47,000. The monthly payment
on the debts was $1856. His total monthly payments were $4430.
Needless to say, he was struggling.*

*Now, since he wasn't escrowing, he wasn't able to pay his taxes. He
had fallen behind and he owed over $16,000. He had a credit score
of 550, which means he's a true non-conforming or sub-prime loan.
He needed help so I created plan for him, what I do is I call it a two-
step plan.*

*We created a new loan of $483,000, paid off the car loans, the credit
card debt, and paid the $16,000 in back taxes, and I gave him $9,000
in cash. I like to make sure my clients have a cash cushion. It's very,
very important to have that cash cushion as you're going to see.*

*Now, because his scores were so low, remember, I told you he was a
550, I felt it was in his best interest to do a two step process. Step
number one was the new loan of $483,000, I needed to keep his
payments as low as possible, so I put him in a forty year term. The
rate was 8.45%, which sounds pretty high, but again, he had a 550
score.*

The new payment with taxes and insurance was $4,391, which was $39 less than he was paying for all his debt and mortgages.

This was still a little bit of a struggle for him. So, we used some of that $9,000 that we took out in cash to help pay the shortfall. This was a two year adjustable, which means it's fixed for two years, and then it will adjust. I know we don't like short term adjustable loans but I had the plan of refinancing it in six months to a year. A fixed rate mortgage at the time would've been over nine percent in his present situation.

After six months to a year of paying everything on time, his scores jumped to the mid 600s. Now, this was a very tight loan, and he was going to have a hard time paying the loan and staying in it for very long. We understood that, and I planned for it. I created a plan over the next six months to work with him, the credit bureaus and his creditors to make sure his credit report was cleaned up and accurate.

The cash out helped him stay current on his new payments, so even if he was short one month or a few months, he had that cushion.

Now comes the second step. After a year, even though rates jumped up a full half percent, since he stayed current, which based on everything I worked out for him, he had no problem doing he fit into a new loan of $505,000 with a rate of 6.5, giving him a thirty year *term. That lowered his monthly payments to $4,061 with taxes and insurance. That's $330 per month less, and a thirty year term instead of a forty year term.*

Now, if he wanted to stay with the forty year term, his rate would be a little bit higher around 6.75. His payment though, would be $3915 with taxes and insurance and that's $476 per month savings.

Now, I know you're thinking, "Well, two loans. He's paying closing costs twice. This is costing him a fortune." Well, that's very true. It is. This was a very expensive process for him, but what were his alternatives? His credit was shot. He couldn't borrow money on credit cards. He was behind in his taxes and couldn't pay them, nor would he be able to pay them in the future.

This two step process put him back in control of his finances and his home. His only other option was to sell the home, which he didn't want to do, or keep going the same way he was going and lose the home, and that certainly was not an option.

James had a happy ending. The plan worked for him and today he is in a new loan with lower payments and in control of his finances. Credit challenges can limit your options but working with a professional you can change your situation. However, you can see that it's far better to avoid those challenges by taking care of debt and credit and not allowing it to get out of control.

Adjustable Rate Mortgages - Overview

Each week we hear more news about the real estate market. The nationwide real estate boom of recent years has given way to what many are predicting will be a full fledged recession. Economists and regulators are questioning the role that mortgage lenders played in helping to create an overheated housing environment.

In the early 2000s, the economy was healthy. Interest rates were low, and consumers felt a bit flush, all of which helped push real estate values up across the country. With values escalating, lenders felt more confident about making mortgages to customers whose poor credit histories had prevented them from buying homes in the past.

When values are rising, borrowers are less likely to default because they can always take money out of their homes or sell it if they run into trouble. That put more potential homebuyers in the market, helping to raise home ownership rates to a record 69% in 2004, which pushed housing prices up more. Skyrocketing prices lured real estate speculators, creating even more demand and driving the cycle further.

To attract this growing pool of borrowers, lenders repurposed creative financing products that had previously been marketed to high income borrowers seeking flexibility with their money. Among the most popular were variations of the adjustable rate mortgage or ARM.

Adjustable rate mortgages are loans whose interest rates adjust up or down periodically. The initial rate is typically a fixed rate for a period of two or three years. The benefit is that the starter rates are lower for adjustable rate mortgages than for traditional fixed rate mortgages. That means lower monthly payments making home ownership more affordable and allowing borrowers to qualify for a bigger loan.

Some of the creative adjustable rate mortgage products that flourished in recent years included "interest only" and "payment option" loans. With the former, a borrower only pays the interest on the loan, not the principle balance during the introductory period. With the payment option ARMs, borrowers get to choose how much they pay each month, enough to cover interest plus principle, the interest only or less than the interest.

Now, in that last scenario the unpaid interest is tacked on to the principal leaving the borrowers owing more than the amount of the original loan. Not the best loan unless you're a very savvy investor.

How prevalent were these loans? Well, nearly 23% of all mortgages taken out in 2005 were interest only adjustable rate mortgages, and more than eight percent were payment option ARMs, according to First American Loan Performance.

In certain once sizzling markets, the numbers were much higher. For example, 34% of all new mortgages in California in 2005 were interest only. These products made sense to borrowers who thought they'd live in the home for a few years, and then sell it for profit or refinance, but now that the housing sales have stalled and prices are softening, borrowers can't do either very easily.

Many borrowers are facing painful payment hikes. According to First American Core Logic study, one third of adjustable rate mortgages taken out between 2004 and 2006 began with teaser rates below four percent. "Payments on these loans will double on average if they haven't already done so," said study author Dr. Christopher Kegan.

Then, there were the loans to borrowers with poor credit. These loans are referred to as sub-prime loans. Sub-prime loans expanded to 20% of the mortgage market in 2006, from nine percent a decade earlier. These loans carry higher interest rates to compensate for the risk posed by borrowers with less than stellar credit. They can be traditional, fixed rate loans, but most are adjustable rate mortgages according to Susan Mockter of the University of Pennsylvania Wharton School.

My personal experience also validates that this is true. About 50% or more of these sub-prime loans happen to be adjustable rate mortgages. Recent sub-prime loans were rife with risky terms, and interest only payment option penalties for paying off the loan early, which makes it costly to refinance to a better loan.

Many of these loans were also low documentation (known as "liar loans" within the industry.) Low documentation requirements mean borrowers needed little paperwork, if anything, to verify that they could in fact afford the loans. These so-called liar loans accounted for about 58% of all loans in 2006, according to First American Loan Performance. So, more than half the loans in 2006 were stated income, no income verification or something along the lines of no proof that you can actually afford these things.

What all of this means is that there's been and will continue to be a rise in foreclosures, and ever tightening mortgage lending guidelines. Now, according to Mortgage Lender Implode, an industry website, more than 63 national mortgage lenders have gone under since late 2006.

We now have fewer lenders to make loans for non-prime borrowers, or borrowers with credit challenges. It's just one more reason why you really need to be very careful of who you work with in the mortgage process.

Your Guide to Adjustable Rate Mortgages

There's been a lot of bad press about adjustable rate mortgages but there is another perspective. The bad press about the market and ARMs can drive people to make decisions. For example, earlier this year there was news that there were a significant number of "cash out refinances" and it was strictly due to the fear of people's adjustable rate mortgages adjusting upward. People were feeling that they had to refinance out of their adjustable rate mortgages and to get a fixed rate mortgage, they had to be locked in before things took a bad turn.

However, studies demonstrate that adjustable rate mortgages will actually outperform fixed rate mortgages, if both mortgages were taken out at the same time and held to term. So, obviously, if you could do better in the adjustable rate mortgage, why would anybody take out a fixed rate mortgage?

There has been a lot of bad information about many things in the industry including adjustable rate mortgages. The news has played on fear but the whole story has not been presented.

So, the consumer, unfortunately, doesn't understand how adjustable rate mortgages work, unfortunately even worse, many loan officers have no idea how adjustable rate mortgages work.

So let's talk a little about how adjustable rate mortgages work. Each adjustable rate mortgage has its own quirks and details, but I'll provide you with a overview that will help you understand how they work.

First of all, what is an adjustable rate mortgage? Obviously, it's something that can adjust over time. Now, there are limits to these adjustments. For example, there's a maximum amount the loan can move up or down. Yes, adjustable rate mortgages can actually go down.

So, let's say for example, there is a one percent adjustment per period. What's a period? Well, a period could be one month. It could be six months. It could be twelve months. It could be more than that, but that gives you a good idea. The periods and adjustments are all established in the loan contract.

There's also something called the lifetime adjustment, or lifetime cap, which is the maximum total adjustment over the life of the loan, and usually that's between five and seven percent from the start rate.

Many people have come to believe that the rates just keep going up forever. Well, it doesn't work that way. Again, there are caps. So, for example, if you have a start rate of four percent and it's a five percent lifetime cap, the maximum your rate can ever go to is nine percent. So, there's no problem there. It can't go to ten. It can't go to eleven. It can't go to twelve, and conversely it can go down to as much as five

Obviously, the bank's not going to go into a negative position and start paying you money, but it can go down. That alone is a huge misconception about adjustable rate mortgages.

There are many different types of adjustable rate mortgages. The adjustment periods can vary from one month to three years and more, the cap will vary and even the first adjustment period can be delayed. For example, you have what's called the monthly ARM, the monthly ARM which is usually based on the 11th District Cost of

Funds Index (COFI), London InterBank Offered Rate (LIBOR), or a Moving Average of monthly values of One-year Treasuries (called MTA or sometimes 12-MAT). Monthly ARMs will typically have a very short fixed initial interest period typically from three to six months. After your initial fixed period, your rate will adjust up or down as the index changes. In a monthly ARM, your monthly payment will also fluctuate. The fluctuations are dependent on the index basis. For example, COFI is one of the slowest moving indices with changes of only a small fraction of a percent at one time. By comparison the one year Treasury is much more volatile.

The option ARM has a low introductory rate, low initial monthly payments and low qualifying rates so that you can qualify for more home. With the option ARM, you have a minimum monthly payment option which is set for 12 months at your initial interest rate. You can pay the minimum or you can pay more. If the minimum is not enough to cover interest you can defer the interest by selecting an interest only option. The option ARM allows you to pay more to speed up the payoff or pay less if you need to keep monthly payments low.

The other ARM s a little bit more common. It's the home equity line of credit. Now, both the monthly and home equity types of loans could adjust on a monthly basis, up or down, or they could stay the same, but they have the ability to adjust every single month.

There are fixed period or hybrid ARMs. Now, these are generally considered the most common types of these types of loans, and basically what it means is that they're fixed for a certain period of time, and then they adjust.

So, for example, maybe you have a two year adjustable, so it's fixed for two years, and then it can adjust, or three year adjustable, fixed for three years and then it adjusts, five year adjustable, fixed for five years and adjusts, seven year adjustable, ten year adjustable. They all work the same way. They're fixed for that short period of time, and then they can adjust, not necessarily up. They can go down.

Unfortunately, many loan officers try to sell these as fixed rate loans, and that is where it begins to falls under the predatory rules. These are not thirty year fixed rate loans. They're thirty year loans, fixed for a period of time.

For many people the adjustment period strikes fear. After all we only hear the bad news about upward adjustments and how it has made the payments unaffordable for homeowners. This has led many to think that the rate can just keep going up and it's unlimited, and that it can only go up, but never go down. In fact many ARMs do adjust down.

This causes many homeowners to panic before readjusting and being seek refinancing before it adjusts. "Oh, I've got to refinance. It's going to adjust. What if it goes up?" They feel they can't afford it. You hear this all the time. I've gotten phone calls from people who have had an adjustable rate mortgage for only six months and they're panicked about the rate adjustment that will happen in five years! That's five years from now, relax.

But, again, the fear is based on the unknown. It's important to understand how adjustable rate mortgages work because they are a very good loan for the right person.

First of all, all adjustable rate mortgages have a start rate. That start rate is usually a teaser rate. It's lower than the fully indexed rate, and it's usually lower than a fixed rate. Again, it's a teaser rate because the fully indexed rate, which I'll explain in a second would be the highest it could go at that given moment.

Now, what does fully indexed mean? All adjustable rate mortgages have two parts to get the adjustable rate. You have an index and you have a margin. The easiest part to understand is the margin. Basically, what the lender does is they figure out what the risk of the loan is, what their profit margin should be, and they create a margin, and it's a fixed number. It never changes.

What you do is you add that index to the margin to figure out your new adjusted rate. Now, where people get confused is they don't understand why it is what it is. So, the best way to describe it is…do you remember when you were in school, you were taught about Pi in math. What was Pi? It was this little character Π, and its value was 3.14.

Why? What did your teacher tell you? It just is. That's what it is. Don't try to figure out. It's just 3.14, and if accepted it, you moved on. Same with the margin, the margin is what the margin is.

You have an index. The index is the adjustable part of the loan. This is the part that can go up and down. It could be a one year Treasury bill. It can be the LIBOR (London Interbank Offered Rate), which is very similar to prime. Basically, if you laid the graph over each other, you'd see that prime and LIBOR pretty much follow each other.

You have what's called a twelve month treasury average, and basically they take the one year treasury and add each month twelve months in a row. Then they average it out over 12 months. That's how they come up with the twelve month treasury average.

Let's look at an example. You have a one-year ARM at 5.75% and that interest rate is fixed for the first year. When your introductory period comes to a close, your lender takes the value of the index – for example, 5.25% -- and adds a margin of 2.75% to arrive at your new interest rate.

So, your calculation is structured like this: 5.25% + 2.75% = 8.00%

However, your loan has a multiple caps. One is the adjustment cap so your current rate plus your adjustment cap is the maximum that you can be charged on the first adjustment by the terms of your contract. So:

Current Rate + Adjustment Cap = Maximum New Rate for this adjustment.

Which calculates as 5.75% + 2.00% = 7.75%   maximum new rate.

In this example, your current interest rate is 5.75%, and your loan has a cap rate of two percentage points. 5.75% + 2.00% = 7.75%. This means that your interest cannot go any higher than 7.75

What happens to the difference? Well, the rest is simply discarded until your next adjustment.

There is also a lifetime cap. This is the maximum increase over the life of the loan. So...

Those are just a few of the most common of the indices. It's really not important what they are per se, as long as they're listed in the Wall Street Journal or New York Times or something that can be tracked so you know exactly what's going on with your loan. To get the fully indexed rate, you want to add the index and the margin together.

Now, how does the rate adjust? Well, let's use the example of the one year adjustable period. One month before the loan adjusts, you get a notice of the new rate. You take the index at the time and you add it to the margin to get that rate.

One month later, if rates jump up one percent, it doesn't matter. Your new payment is based on that notice. So, it doesn't matter what happens in a month or two months from now. Conversely, if rates go down, you're still locked into what is now a higher rate. It won't go down for you.

How does the payment adjust? At the adjustment period, the loan does what's called recasts. Basically, what that means is that your payment is going to be based on the balance of the loan at the time. They take the new rate, whatever that new adjusted rate will be and the balance of the term.

As an example, if you're in a five year adjustable, at the fifth year, start of the sixth year, your rate is going to adjust from five percent to let's say six percent. The monthly payment will be based on the amount of money needed to pay off the loan in 25 years at six percent, rather than the initial 30 year term.

One of the big advantages of an adjustable rate mortgage is instead of actually refinancing your adjustable rate mortgage and incurring costs, you can actually pay the loan down. So, right before it recasts, if the rate is going to go up, you can pay the loan down. By paying it down by $10,000, $20,000, or $50,000, you will lower the balance to be recast, thus lowering your payment needed to pay off the loan over the balance of the term. Using this strategy, your payment might actually go down. While I am not proposing this as a solution for everyone it could conceivably be cheaper than simply refinancing the loan.

Why Consider an Adjustable Rate Mortgage?

Now that you have an overview of ARMs, why would why would anybody choose to take out an adjustable rate mortgage? Well, let's say you're only going to be in the loan for a short period of time. It would certainly pay. I would liken it to a car lease. You're leasing a car for two years.

Would you take out a five year extended warranty? Of course you wouldn't. Why wouldn't you? Well, you're not going to have the car for more than two years. Why would you want to pay for a five year extended warranty?

In the same way, why take out a thirty year fixed rate loan, if you won't have the loan past three, five or seven years? It doesn't make any sense especially if an adjustable rate mortgage is going to be cheaper.

There are many reasons to take out adjustable rate mortgages. An adjustable rate mortgage is going to typically be cheaper than a fixed rate mortgage. For example, a five year adjustable rate mortgage usually is going to be half to three-quarters of a percent cheaper than a thirty year fixed. A three year adjustable rate mortgage is usually between three-quarters and as much one percent cheaper than a thirty year fixed.

Let's look at a few reasons people select adjustable rate mortgages.

Cash flow. You need money. Maybe you're starting a business and you want nice low payments in the beginning because your business cash flow is low. You need to build your business up, and in three to five years, you're really confident that your business is going to take off and you're going to make some good money.

You may not need to refinance depending upon where rates are at the time. Maybe rates will be lower in three to five years, and you won't have to refinance. Your payments will actually be lower. Maybe your rate will be the same, no real change in payments. Maybe your rate will be higher, but how much higher? It may be so little that it's really not worth the costs, plus if you're making more money, you may be able to afford the higher payment and why bother refinancing?

Planning to Sell. Perhaps you're thinking ahead that you want to sell the house in three to five years. Do you really want to take out a thirty year fixed? Why would you want to have a higher rate when you know you're getting rid of that home in three to five years?

Debt. You've run into some financial trouble and you're behind in your mortgage. You need to catch up on the mortgage, and you're late with some other bills. You also need a cash cushion, some sort of reserve.

You don't qualify for a conforming loan, due to your low overall credit rating, and you need a year or two years for your credit scores to come up. Which paying off your debt should help to accomplish. You take out a short term, two year adjustable, since it offers the lowest rate. You know you're going to be refinancing out of it in a year or two.

Income Will Increase. You're buying a home now but in three to five years, you're going to have big gains in your salary or your income. Maybe you're a teacher and you're going to reach tenure, which will give you a big pay increase. Or maybe you work for the government and one of the contracts with the government says you're going to have a big pay increase in a few years.

Well, it's great to start with a low rate five year adjustable rate mortgage, which will allow you to afford the loan now knowing that you're going to have more income in a few years. When the adjustable rate mortgage adjusts, you should be making enough to pay the increase.

First Home. Let's say you're buying a starter home, and you plan to move into a bigger home in three to seven years. In fact my wife Wendy and I learned this lesson the hard way. We bought our first house planning on moving in five years, but I made a big mistake. I took out a thirty year fixed rate loan. I should've known better, but…I didn't. We all live and learn.   Now, if a professional mortgage planner could make a mistake on his own mortgage, How can you expect to plan your own mortgage. It doesn't make sense. I let fear dictate what I did, so I understand where you're coming from if you have fear about adjustable rate mortgages.

Of course, when we bought our new house, we did it a little bit differently. I learned my lesson. I took out an adjustable rate mortgage. In my case, the rate was half a percent lower than the thirty year fixed rate.

Move around a lot. Now, let's say you have a job that moves you around a lot. I had a client that worked for JC Penney, and his job was to open new stores or improve existing stores. So, he'd move to the area and open a store, turn an existing store around or close it. Then, he'd move onto the next area.

He only stayed in the home for two to four years. So, we always used an adjustable rate mortgage, a three year adjustable rate mortgage to be specific. Even if he ended up in that loan for four years and in year four it actually went up, he could afford the higher payment due to the huge savings he had over the first three years.

Refinancing Adjustable Rate Mortgages

How do you determine if you should refinance your adjustable rate mortgage? In the past few years there's been a lot of news about people refinancing their adjustable rate mortgages, and you really need to determine a few things.

First of all, is it a sub-prime loan? I personally don't like calling them sub-prime, but it is the term that's used. I like calling them non-conforming loans. Why is that important?

Well, these types of adjustable rate mortgages are designed to strictly go up. They do not go down. The floor rate is the start rate. What is the floor rate? It is the lowest rate the mortgage can go down to. That's called the floor.

On non-conforming loans, the floor rate is the start rate, and, in most cases, they can never go below the start rate. Now, most of these adjustable rate mortgages have a four to seven percent margin. If your index is LIBOR, London Interbank Offered Rate, which as of this writing is over five, even if your margin is only four, your loan is going to go to nine percent at some point.

Now, if you started out at nine percent, you're not going to have to worry about it. You're not going to go up, but, I would recommend looking into a refinance if you're at nine percent.

Basically, these loans were designed to be refinanced when they adjust. That's the way they were designed. The lenders expect them to be refinanced within the two or three year period whatever the term of the fixed rate period is. The expectation is they'll be refinanced out.

So, again, if it's a sub-prime or non-conforming loan, you almost definitely want to refinance. To figure out whether or not you want to refinance your adjustable rate mortgage if it's a conforming type of loan, it's a little more complicated because these adjustable rate mortgages are designed to go up and down.

Again, there's a floor rate on all adjustable loans, but in the case of a conforming loan, the margin is the floor rate, and technically you can go down to 2.75 if that's what your margin is.

Now, for example, if interest rates were to go down to the level they were in November of 2004, your rate could go down on an adjustable rate mortgage to as low as four and three quarters. So, again, would you want to refinance out of a 4 ¾ rate? Probably not.

You need to determine the cost to refinance. If rates only went up, it might take you two to three years to save the costs of your refinance. You really want to meet with a professional mortgage planner to determine your needs. You need a copy of your note so we can understand the terms of the existing loan, what you're looking for, what your goals and needs are. Don't just decide to refinance your adjustable rate mortgage because of fear.

To Help You Understand More About Mortgage Financing I have Developed a CD titled…

Understanding The Good Faith Estimate

To receive a FREE Copy of this information packed CD go to
www.GFE.yourhomeyourmoney.org

Glossary of Loan Terms

Amortization: The repayment of a mortgage loan through monthly installments of principal and interest. The monthly payment amount is based on a schedule that will allow you to own your home at the end of a specific time period (for example, 15 or 30 years).

Annual Percentage Rate (APR): The APR is calculated by using a standard formula and shows the cost of a loan. It is expressed as a yearly interest rate and includes the interest, points, mortgage insurance, and other fees associated with the loan.

Application: The loan application is a form that is used to collect important information about the potential borrower which is necessary to the loan underwriting process. The application is the first step in the loan approval process.

Appraisal: An appraisal is a documented estimate of a home's fair market value. It is generally required by lenders before the mortgage loan is approved to ensure that the loan amount does not exceed the property value.

Appraiser: A qualified and licensed professional who uses his or her experience and knowledge to prepare the appraisal estimate.

ARM: Adjustable Rate Mortgage is a mortgage loan subject to changes in interest rates. ARM monthly payments increase or decrease at intervals determined by the lender. The change in the monthly payment is usually subject to a cap that is outlined in the loan documentation.

Assessor: A government official who is responsible for determining the value of a property for the purpose of taxation.

Assumable mortgage: This is a mortgage that can be transferred from a seller to a buyer. Once the loan has been assumed by the buyer the seller is no longer responsible for repaying it. The transfer of an assumable mortgage will typically involve fees and/or a credit package.

Balloon Mortgage: A mortgage that typically offers low rates for an initial period of time (usually 5, 7, or 10) years and after that time period elapses, the balance is due or is refinanced by the borrower.

Bankruptcy: A federal law where a person's assets are turned over to a trustee and used to pay off outstanding debts.

Borrower: A person who has been approved to receive a loan and is then obligated to repay it and any additional fees according to the loan terms.

Budget: A detailed record of all income earned and spent during a specific period of time.

Cap: This refers to a limit, such as that placed on an adjustable rate mortgage, on how much a monthly payment or interest rate can increase or decrease.

Cash reserves: A cash amount sometimes required to be held in reserve in addition to the down payment and closing costs. The amount of the reserve is determined by the lender.

Certificate of title: This document is provided by a qualified source, such as a title company and shows that the property legally belongs to the current owner. Certificates of title are checked for liens and claims before the title is transferred at closing.

Closing: The closing is also referred to as settlement and is the time when the property is formally sold and transferred from the seller to the buyer. At the closing, the borrower takes on the loan obligation, signs documentation, pays all closing costs, and receives title from the seller.

Closing costs: These costs are above and beyond the sales prices and may include title fees, escrow fees, first loan payment, loan costs, etc. These costs generally vary by geographic location and are typically detailed to the borrower after submission of a loan application.

Conventional loan: A loan that is not guaranteed or insured by the government.

Credit history: History of an individual's debt payment and is used by lenders to gauge a potential borrower's ability to repay a loan.

Credit report: A documentation of an individual's credit history that lists past and present debts, timeliness of payments, past and current employers and residences.

Debt-to-income ratio: A comparison of gross income to housing and non-housing expenses. It is generally recommended that the monthly mortgage payment should be no more than 28% of monthly gross income and the mortgage payment combined with non-housing debts should not exceed 40% of income.

Deed: The document that transfers ownership of a property.

Deed-in-lieu: A deed is given to the lender, in lieu of foreclosure, to fulfill the obligation to repay the debt. While the process doesn't allow the borrower to remain in the house it does help avoid the costs, time, and effort associated with foreclosure.

Default: The inability to pay monthly mortgage payments in a timely manner or to otherwise meet the mortgage terms.

Delinquency: Failure of a borrower to make timely mortgage payments under a loan agreement.

Discount point: This is normally paid at closing and generally calculated to be equivalent to 1% of the total loan amount, discount points are paid to reduce the interest rate on a loan.

Down payment: The upfront payment that is paid toward the home's purchase price and is not part of the mortgage loan. Down payments can vary from 0 to 25% of the home's purchase price.

Earnest money: This is money put down by a potential buyer to show that he or she is serious about purchasing the home. It becomes part of the down payment if the offer is accepted, is returned if the offer is rejected, or is forfeited if the buyer pulls out of the deal.

EEM: Energy Efficient Mortgage is an FHA program that helps homebuyers save money on utility bills by enabling them to finance the cost of adding energy efficiency features to a new or existing home as part of the home purchase

Equity: This represents a homeowner's financial interest in a property and is calculated by subtracting the amount still owed on the mortgage from the fair market value of the property.

Escrow account: A separate account into which the lender puts a portion of each monthly mortgage payment. Expenses such as property taxes, homeowners insurance, mortgage insurance, etc. are paid from the escrow account.

Fair Housing Act: Law that prohibits discrimination in all facets of the home buying process on the basis of race, color, national origin, religion, sex, familial status, or disability.

Fannie Mae: Federal National Mortgage Association (FNMA is a federally-chartered enterprise owned by private stockholders that purchases residential mortgages and converts them into securities for sale to investors. By purchasing mortgages, Fannie Mae supplies funds that lenders may loan to potential homebuyers.

FHA: Federal Housing Administration. Established in 1934 to advance homeownership opportunities for all Americans, FHA assists homebuyers by providing mortgage insurance to lenders to cover most losses that may occur when a borrower defaults. This encourages lenders to make loans to borrowers who might not qualify for conventional mortgages.

Fixed-rate mortgage: A mortgage in which the payments remain the same throughout the life of the loan because the interest rate and other terms are fixed and do not change.

Flood insurance: Insurance that protects homeowners against losses from a flood. The lender will require flood insurance before approving a loan for homes located in flood zones.

Foreclosure: Legal process in which mortgaged property is sold to pay the loan of the defaulting borrower.

Freddie Mac: Federal Home Loan Mortgage Corporation (FHLM) is a federally-chartered corporation that purchases residential mortgages, securitizes them, and sells them to investors; this provides lenders with funds for new homebuyers.

Ginnie Mae: Government National Mortgage Association (GNMA). Government-owned Corporation overseen by the U.S. Department of Housing and Urban Development, Ginnie Mae pools FHA-insured and VA-guaranteed loans to back securities for private investment; as With Fannie Mae and Freddie Mac, the investment income provides funding that may then be lent to eligible borrowers by lenders.

Good faith estimate: This is an estimate of all closing fees including pre-paid and escrow items as well as lender charges. Good faith estimates must be given to the borrower within three days after submission of a loan application.

Home inspection: An examination of the structure and mechanical systems to determine a home's safety and makes the potential homebuyer aware of any repairs that may be needed.

Home warranty: Offers protection for mechanical systems and attached appliances against unexpected repairs not covered by homeowner's insurance.

Homeowner's insurance: Insurance policy that protects the homeowner from damage to the dwelling and its contents.

Homeowner's insurance can include specific coverage for damage from floods, fires, earthquakes, theft, etc. This insurance can also protect homeowners from claims against them for damage or injury that occurs on the property.

HUD: U.S. Department of Housing and Urban Development. Agency established in 1965, HUD works to create a decent home and suitable living environment for all Americans; it does this by addressing housing needs, improving and developing American communities, and enforcing fair housing laws.

HUD1 Statement: Also known as the "settlement sheet," it itemizes all closing costs; must be given to the borrower at or before closing.

HVAC: Heating, Ventilation and Air Conditioning; a home's heating and cooling system.

Index: Measurement used by lenders to determine changes to the Interest rate charged on an adjustable rate mortgage.

Interest: Cost of borrowing money expressed as a percentage of the amount borrowed.

Insurance: Protection against a specific loss over a period of time that is secured by the payment of a regularly scheduled premium.

Introductory Rate: Also known as a teaser rate. Some loans have a lower introductory interest rate, which is in effect for a limited time. At the end of the introductory period, the interest rate will increase.

Lien: A legal claim against property that must be satisfied when the property is sold. Typically liens are for mortgage, taxes or judgments.

Loan: Money borrowed that is usually repaid with interest.

Loan-to-value (LTV) ratio: A percentage calculated by dividing the amount borrowed by the price or appraised value of the home to be purchased. The higher the LTV, the less cash a borrower is required to pay as down payment.

Lock-in: As interest rates can change frequently, many lenders offer an interest rate lock-in that guarantees a specific interest rate if the loan is closed within a specific time.

Loan Term: Length of time until your loan is due and payable.

Margin: An amount the lender adds to an index to determine the interest rate on an adjustable rate mortgage.

Mortgage: A lien on the property that secures the promise to repay a loan.

Mortgage insurance: Policy that protects lenders against some or most of the losses that can occur when a borrower defaults on a mortgage loan. Mortgage insurance is required primarily for borrowers with a down payment of less than 20% of the home's purchase price.

Mortgage insurance premium (MIP): a monthly payment that is usually part of the mortgage payment which is paid by a borrower for mortgage insurance.

Offer: Generally in writing and indicates a potential buyer's willingness to purchase a home at a specific price.

Origination: Refers to the process of preparing, submitting, and evaluating a loan application. Loan origination generally includes a credit check, verification of employment, and a property appraisal.

Origination fee: The charge for originating a loan. It is usually calculated in the form of points and paid at closing.

PITI: Principal, Interest, Taxes, and Insurance – These are the four elements of a monthly mortgage payment; payments of principal and interest go directly towards repaying the loan while the portion that covers taxes and insurance (homeowner's and mortgage, if applicable) goes into an escrow account to cover the fees when they are due.

PMI, Private Mortgage Insurance: Privately-owned companies that offer standard and special affordable mortgage insurance programs for qualified borrowers with down payments of less than 20% of a purchase price.

Pre-approve: The lender commits to lend to a potential borrower and the commitment remains as long as the borrower still meets the qualification requirements at the time of purchase.

Pre-foreclosure sale: Allows a defaulting borrower to sell the mortgaged property to satisfy the loan and avoid foreclosure.

Pre-qualify: Informal process in which a lender determines the maximum amount an individual is eligible to borrow. Pre-qualification does not include a credit check and is not a pre-approval for a loan.

Prepayment: Payment of the mortgage loan before the scheduled due date. Prepayment may be subject to penalty fee.

Principal: The amount borrowed from a lender and does not include interest or additional fees.

Rehabilitation mortgage: A mortgage that covers the costs of rehabilitating (repairing or Improving) a property. Some rehabilitation mortgages such as the FHA's 203(k) enable borrowers to roll the costs of rehabilitation and home purchase into one mortgage loan.

RESPA, Real Estate Settlement Procedures Act: A law protecting consumers from abuses during the residential real estate purchase and loan process by requiring lenders to disclose all settlement costs, practices, and relationships.

Settlement: Also called closing. Time in which the property transfers from seller to buyer.

Title 1: FHA-insured loan that allows a borrower to make non-luxury improvements (like renovations or repairs) to their home.

Title insurance: Insurance that protects the lender against any claims that arise from arguments about ownership of the property. Title insurance is also available for homebuyers.

Title search: A check of public records to ensure that the seller is the recognized owner of the real estate and that there are no unsettled liens or other claims against the property.

Truth-in-Lending: Federal law obligating a lender to give full written disclosure of all fees, terms, and conditions associated with the loan initial period and then adjusts to another rate that lasts for the term of the loan.

Underwriting: The process of analyzing a loan application to determine the amount of risk involved in making the loan. The underwriting process includes a review of the potential borrower's credit history and a judgment of the property value.